ACKNOWLEDGMENTS

A sincere humble thank you to the people that recognized and nurtured my talent at a very young age: Shqiponja and Haki Baçi. Thank you for believing in me, even when I stopped believing in myself.

Thank you to Prof. Dr. B.Gaçe, Prof. Dr. V. Memisha, Prof. Dr. J. Spaho, Prof. Dr. Rusi, Prof. Dr. Shyta and Prof. T.Topalli for the warm welcome they have given to my poetry and their support.

A special thank you to my dear friend Marisa Ashiku for being a great moral support and a part of my journey by helping me with the visual presentations of my poetry online.

Thanks to Iva Poshnjari for editing this book with great patience and to Arbëresh Dalipi for designing the cover and online publishing.

Thanks to all my fans and supporters that read me all over the world and inspire me with their comments to move forward. It's nice to know that I'm being heard and that what I say matters to the world.

Contents

A Bunch of

Poems

Instead of Flowers

ARMENIDA QYQJA

Armenida Qyqja

THE TEARS OF TIME

Left on the ceiling are the tears of time,

Faint marks that under the voice complain to the oblivion,

On the fireplace, the burned out coal,

Holds monologueswith silence, about abandonment…

Now, you entirely, lay on my hand,

As gray haired I wander in the world,

Inside the tired walls, you keep the voices of a whole life

And I, inside of my fist, keep the key to the gate…

(Feb 2020)

BREATH IN ME

You came to remind the flame
Of all its forgotten colours, again,
Light breeze that with the summer's sun
Endlessly covers my hair in kisses...

Breath, breath in me love,
I'm not afraid of getting all burned out,
Let's see how high we can go,
Will the gods in Olympus be jealous of us?!

Give me a little blue from your eyes, my dear,
Throw it into the rose of lips,
Into the green that my eyes hide deep in,
Breath in me, let's get higher with each kiss...
(July 2022)

I DROWN IN THE TEAR DROP

Inside the frame of your eyes I lay,

My light weight, the walls support,

Above me, time hangs over the arch of dreams,

The light pours down over me…

The dimensions expand,

The frame walls bend,

Me and the universe inside your eyes…

In the tear drop I drown, and I'm born again,

Pain and kisses,

Wave...after wave...again…

(Feb 2020)

PEOPLE'S PARADOX

Ah, that's how the world is,

It fears the sneezes,

The tails of the comets,

The bloody moons,

The rounding of the new millenniums…

Then forgets about all the earthquakes and plagues,

And declares itself immortal

While playing with the arms of the atomic clock…

Ah, that's how the world is,

It cries and laughs, sticking its tongue out,

It screams and plays out every trick,

And then starts to mock Atlas

That keeps carrying it on his shoulders,

While being kicked by it,

Noah's ark,

The regretful Einstein,

And the genius that while shivering on his deathbed

  Wrote: "Requiem..."

(Feb 2020)

COME, WITH WHITE WINGS

Another day closed inside my chest,

Painfully, like the wings of a swan

When their whiteness is soiled by darkness,

Lowering its head down…

Huddling, somewhere, among leaves,

Waiting for tomorrow…

My tomorrow, come!

Numb are the wings of the dreams

In this starless, wet sky…

Useless are the lights of the towers,

From the thirtieth floors uselessly

They stretch their heads,

The stars can never be reached

Or substituted…

Come, my tomorrow!

Come with white wings of love

From the far sky

And kiss my tears,

Dreams that shine like lights lay in my eyes…

(Feb 2020)

Armenida Qyqja

WEAR THE SMILE ON YOUR FACE

Emptiness expands inside my lungs,

When you lock yourself in silence,

I don't know what hurts you: the past or the present,

That keeps playing the masquerade ball…

A bitter taste the vacuum leaves behind,

And pale yellow autumn look,

Patience sweetheart, it's still mid-august,

There are still some summer days in the calendar…

Leave the devils behind their masks,

Wrap your body onto mine and hold on tight,

Take the dreams from my eyes

And wear the smile on your face…

(Aug 2022)

A TIME FULL OF NOISE

I turned everything down, even the lights,

Shutting outside the world and the noise…

On the flat screens

The news shivered with flu's fever,

Forgetting all about the fires and the bombs…

And just like this, news fills in for news,

Burying the previous in the archives,

Outside on the street

A barefooted, war escapee coughs,

By a dock, someone mourns a drowned loved one…

I turned everything down,

Silent may the noise be for a while,

Under the dust of the oblivion, nothing can sleep,

In anguish moans and curses

   The wicked time…

(Feb 2020)

LET ME IN

In the white foam we melted the kisses,

Seagulls and white veils of clouds they became,

Feelings that slammed against the gates of the soul,

"Let me in" kept saying to me with your lips…

The waves kept on crashing on the Ionian cliffs,

Thousands of crystals crumbling into light,

The echo they sowed in the abyss of my heart,

That says "I love you" with every beat and season…

(Feb 2020)

MADLY

You'll never be able to understand

The unstoppable madness of the feeling…

I can't spell out for you love

What is written on each cell…

Even better that you pay no attention to me,

The words have no chance to reach

The messages of thousand neurons,

The kilometers of lights they lighten up…

Even better that you don't read my poems…

Close your eyes and listen to my breath

As it lets itself in your lungs…

Don't ask for explanations! I love you madly…

(Feb 2022)

RELEASE YOUR BREATH

Overcome the doorstep of the foggy dreams,

And come out of the wounded eyes,

On my lips release your breath…

Come, overcome the rough mountain ranges of the wait,

Let go like an avalanche and whiten

The nights and the dark circles under my eyes…

Come! I am there, where the words end

And the knocks begin…

Just listen, my love! It's me…

(Feb 2020)

I WANT TO GROW OLD WITH YOU

Time goes by, and one forgets himself,

The eyes, the cheekbones…

The butterflies of dreams get lost with the sun's rays…

One gets used to the image

That keeps changing on the mirror every second,

With clumsy steps, faded knock,

Hunched shoulders

From the invisible weight of the years…

One betrays himself, my love,

And I feel deep in me, that I want to grow old with you,

Inside your eyes,

I want to lay asleep the image of me today,

My smile…

I love you…

And I don't want to waste time with verb conjugations,

I love you, now and through all the time tenses,

Until my wings fade,

And shall be no longer,

Gone with the last ray of light…

(Jan 2020)

Armenida Qyqja

MY HEARTBEAT
I SEND TO YOU

The clouds whitened my hair with their gray silence,

On the endless escapes…

Seasons that change over my shriveled skin,

Again on the road,

Like an aged migrant traveler…

Cause, my heart doesn't obey me,

And rises over the reasons,

Sending its beat to you while trembling,

A lightening that burns and dies out in pain,

While carrying itself through darkness and rain…

And I try to bring a light with my eyes,

To your sky, that lays wounded by the storms,

A word, a new hope to give to the lips,

To the eyes that wait for me to return…

(March 2020)

THE SUN OF MY DAYS

I chewed the silence, every bit of it,

My teeth went numb from the icy bites,

With them crunched the soul,

Full of pain in every syllable of emptiness,

And again I called you,

And waited for you to abandon Olympus wrapped in

clouds,

With a small flame under your shirt,

From your chest

The gold sun of my days to be born...

(March 2020)

WITH THE VOICE OF MY SOUL

Inside the night's chest, the sighs spin,

And the dreams lose their way through clouds…

A moon that drips over the gray-haired doorstep,

With its fragile rays summons my soul…

Oblivion luxuriates above the gate's arch,

That a knock awaits with longingness through time,

My fist I send with the wings of the heart,

With the voice of my soul I say to you: "I'm here"…

(March 2020)

LIKE AN ODYSSEY

The light of my eyes flickers,

As it breaks over the crest of the tears' waves,

Again, pulsating like the stars, stretches to reach you…

The drowned words carrying on its back,

Wave after wave,

Together with the soul, as the tired arms beat the water…

With your lips bring the shore close to me,

And open up your arms!

Like a lost Odyssey,

I have traveled so much,

  To get to you,

    Love...

(March 2020)

CRAZY JEALOUS!

Far away from me you sleep…

A little longer, a little…

I wait and with you in my mind I kill the long hours,

While like a volcano woken up by the genies,

Jealousy covers me all over,

Jealous of the bed sheets wrapped around your body,

The pillow where your dreams slumber,

Jealous of the rain that sings to you in the dark

background,

Jealous of this weary winter morning…

Jealous, ah, how jealous,

Of the day that will awake very soon next to you,

Of the light that will pour over your body,

Of the streets where your feet will step on,

Jealous, so crazy jealous…!

(Dec 2019)

HOMELAND OF MY LOVE

My love, take my kisses with you,

Nests of dreams weaved by the lips of the soul,

Let them pour out on the streets together with your

footsteps,

To your chest they will return again like birds.

My love, take my eyes everywhere with you,

On the gray of your soul let them pour,

In the pathways, denied of light, let them shine,

Homeland of my love...

    You...

(Jan 2020)

CURFEW AND PRAYER

When sadness tries to isolate you within in its walls,
And by the window, the jasmines inside their buds
Lock their lips and don't say a single word to you,
With the fragile ray that teases in the midst of clouds,
There, I am, from the far distance
    Coming closer, on your shoulders…

A medieval death has frightened the streets for days,
And the walls and fences have tightened their rows,
There, among the torn bodies from the time and the
earthquakes,
There, I am, for you
    A living prayer…
(Mar 2020)

UNDER THE SKIN THE KISSES CRY OUT

Longingness knocks with the humid air,

Gently, with your soft fingers…

I tremble, and flutter in memories,

Just from the touch of your warm eyes.

You come to me like a warm breeze of feelings,

And inside my heart you become a hurricane,

Under the skin your kisses cry out,

Their warmth inside me becomes a volcano...

(Oct 2019)

LOVE ME

My love, love me even when the time

Has no time for us,

There, in a corner of the heart full of storm,

Like a bird wrapped in the gloomy clouds let me be…

Let me fight, fall and rise,

With you,

Let me be close to you!

My love, love me,

The time will always be the same,

Cholera!

(Jun 2019)

EDEN ISN'T LOST

I love you...is as old as the world,

As the stones that raise the walls of the dreams,

DNA block in the blood chain,

Carried over with every rebirth,

I love you again and again…

Archaic feeling that doesn't need new words,

But only the eyes filled with you,

And the lips of soul drunk with the kisses,

The ambrosia stolen from the glasses of the gods,

I love you...Nothing, not a single other word,

Unwritten let them flow,

Through the lowered eyelashes,

To the verses of the feelings,

On them, let the tired Orfeo sleep.

Old, archaic is the feeling…

I love you!

Eden isn't lost...

(Oct 2019)

I'M IN LOVE

We forgot about Ukraine, too,
There on the ashy mountains
Where mothers' sons become statistics,
Even the news has fallen asleep on them…

No, I shall feel no remorse,
I didn't kill or betray Ukraine,
I just got tired of listening and thinking about the war,
It's not my fault I am still so thirsty for life…

No, I shall feel no remorse about anything at all,
Not even my own country that keeps shrinking
Everyone wants to flee, while I…
But we won't talk about this either…

We won't talk about anything out there at all,
We'll just hold each other's gaze in silence,
Dressed only with your smile,
I'll crash on your bare chest, drunk with pleasure…

The hell with the world and its endless troubles,
Its suicides and the endless cries for help,
Behind myself I locked the door tonight,
I am still so much in love with life…
(July 2022)

PETREL OF MY SOUL

Rise above the waves, my petrel,

A free verse become, a song in the storm,

Bird that dies and is reborn again in the foamy sea,

Never surrender to the pain that grows like a mountain!

Raise above the waves, my petrel,

Stretch your fragile wings towards the sky,

With the sun's ray hiding behind the clouds,

Climb through the storm, again to get kissed…!

(Jul 2020)

INSIDE MY HEART YOU BECAME A GOD

Like a fiery meteor shower,

Upon my dark sky you fell,

To turn on again the lights of my soul.

With your warm breath

You woke up the silenced-out heartbeat,

That's why inside of it Prometheus you became, god…

In the long night you came to me,

Like a purple dawn on my fragile shoulders…

On my tear you placed your ember kiss,

Cradle on my murdered-dream eye.

(Aug 2019)

THE PUT OUT KISSES CRY OUT

Solitude rocks me in the cold cradle,

Sleep...Sleep...without awakening,

The pains cry out in the deaf night,

"Sleep...Sleep...without awakening",- they say to me.

You were a miracle, a beautiful vision,

That went, leaving me on the edge of the dream full of

longingness,

A faded kiss, still hungry,

Gurgling words on the lips that without it, are desolate.

In the cradle filled with murderous tears,

Solitude rocks me bitterly,

"Sleep...Sleep...without awakening" saying to me,

The put out kisses cry out in pain

"Sleep...Sleep...without awakening" to me they say...

(Aug 2019)

THE STORM OF WORDS

Your words turn into stones inside my soul,

That treasured you as the most sacred idol,

In the seas of pains, they drowned my fragile heart,

Its last beat they stopped at the dream's gates.

My love, you forgot, the Lord only needed one word,

To create the world in one day,

Just like it was a storm of mixed words,

That stopped the tower's body growing to the gods.

Babel, Babel, hurricane of poisonous words

Crashed down suddenly on the temple of love,

My love, I loved you, ah, how much I still love you,

But now I'm sleeping covered under the snow of words…

(Aug 2019)

THE MIRROR

In your clear eyes, my day awakens,

When your warm gazes land on me,

In the distant edges, the night shrinks defeated,

Together with the doubts and the dark shadows.

In silence you follow around my moves,

And I pretend I don't feel your eyes on my body,

In front the mirror betrays me, as always,

The game of my eyes, reveals to you without words,

secretly…

(Apr 2019)

IF YOU GO…

If you go and with you, you take my dreams,

There would be only dark, torn-light skies floating in my

eyes,

Thousands of long kilometers of emptiness.

And if you take with you the echo of your footsteps,

From the streets of my soul,

After their traces, you'll find my tears…

Translate it, my dear,

Find a dictionary, somewhere,

    And translate it!

There in that endless line,

Its short road,

Thousands of words will tell you…

(Mar 2019)

LIFE'S SONG

On top of the ruins life sings its fragile song,

With the voice of the soul they couldn't kill,

Calling love on the empty windows,

Resting its pain on the blackened walls...

A new day waiting, far from the gray rubbles,

Kisses and smiles again to sprout,

Placing its lips on the open wounds,

To stop the warm blood from flowing out...

The walls keep listening and so do the windows,

The song of life that rises above death,

Willing to give the last thread of breath,

To love again and again and again…

(Apr 2022)

Armenida Qyqja

YOU ARE INSIDE MY EYES

I investigate the silence that has drawn down on us,

The words that try to flee behind its curtain,

The lights, that I don't where they go, to put themselves

out,

Taking with them even the hieroglyphs…

I investigate the shadows that drop on your contours,

The eyebrows, the corners of your lips that smile,

Tell me, my caresses and kisses,

Would they run away from them?

The roads of air tighten, secretly,

The stars escape together with the dreams and hopes,

But not me! I am there!

And you are entirely inside my eyes!

(Apr 2020)

EMPTY DAYS

The days fall on puddles of emptiness,
And in them, the night stares at its own reflection,
I, daughter of the days harvested before their time,
Have no other option, but to fall and rise…

The stolen childhood, like a desired toy,
Away from the hands, in the showcase untouched
remains,
The youth, even worse, torn from the soul,
With the dreams that rip their arms stretching over the
seas…

The moon peaks out its head, somewhere through the
clouds,
Sometimes bloody and sometimes so pale,
A wind that blows, adds wrinkles to the puddle,
In my reflection I feel the shriveling of time…
(Apr 2020)

WAITING

Silence flows on the evening's walls,

Completely whitened from waiting under the moon,

Secretly, chewing the bricks of the soul,

That higher and higher raise the lonely dwelling.

That's how the genesis has been,

For all the fortresses that now sleep,

From the erosion with invisible teeth,

They've had their unavoidable ending…

Wait, wait ground in silence,

Wait, bitterly minced by the wind,

Wait, mixed with tears of pain,

Wait, that brings down the walls of the soul, taking its

bricks away...

(Apr 2019)

I NEED A HEART

Even the greatest empires

Have crumbled into ruins, my love,

Smoke and dust of the oblivion they have become,

Leaving behind their skeletons of stone,

That drip blood and tears through time.

My love, even the greatest heroes have fallen,

Have died and turned to dust like just anyone,

Leaving a song behind from mouth to mouth,

But one day even that can go silent…

My love, I don't need the heroes,

Nor the gods that time has forgotten long time ago,

Tonight I need a heart, the one inside of you,

That can kiss my soul with each beat, through the night…

(Nov 2019)

Armenida Qyqja

THE LIGHT INSIDE MY EYES CALLS YOU

From far distances your gazes come to me,
Soundless cry outs of the soul,
The spaces exchange place, and so do hearts,
The bunker of feelings that holds you inside.

Because the world, always has a cold war cooking and
brewing,
Always with sanctions and embargoes,
Flattering praises, high pedestals,
Monuments of betrayal and murder.

The light inside my eyes calls you,
Tears of blood slowly dripping,
When your voice loses its colour on the way,
When doubts engulf your heart…
(Oct 2019)

SEND ME YOUR SOUL WITH A DREAM

The heart grew tired

Filling in the parts of the dialogs inside of it…

This duplicate of me that can't get enough of you,

Bring to an end with your arrival!

Come, bring calmness to my longingness

In the long sleepless nights,

Come with the dawn,

Sit beside my bed, wildly undone,

With your kisses straighten

Its waves, the white sheets…

In a new dream send me your soul,

Together with you side by side,

On the road that stretches inside the heartbeats…

(May 2022)

A STORM BIRD I AM

My dear, you know that I'm a storm bird,

That sings and cries with the crazy wind,

I know that you wait for me somewhere beyond the

clouds,

And that's why I flap my wings even harder…

And the wind rises, trying to blow me down,

To silence my voice and my journey,

But I know that you wait for me beyond the dark clouds,

That's why even louder, "I love you" I cry out...

(Aug 2019)

THE MIRROR'S ANGRY LOOKS

My own self in the mirror doesn't love me today,

Angrily it looks at me, with dark eyes,

We've argued and all the fault I've laid on you,

And you, on me, all of it, as always…

You know that I'll take it all back, and carry it on my back,

Because without you the mirror gives me angry looks,

The air grinds me with the deaf absence of your voice,

The gray invades my eyes with the clouds of tears.

A tear runs down, leaving a streak behind,

Turning the mascara into a paved road,

So that the words "I love you" can be on the way,

And again on your lips to lay…

(Aug 2019)

TO OTHERS I'M LEAVING OLYMPUS

Dear Tolstoy,

To you, I'm leaving the unbearable pain

For the masterpiece,

To God I am praying

To give me calmness,

I have no need for pedestals,

I just need peace…

A shore I need, a strong rock,

To throw on my tired body,

Enough with the tests,

I am not an offspring of the Titans,

Or of the demi-gods...

Since a long time ago,

To others I have left Olympus...

(Aug 2019)

DON'T ALLOW THE SADNESS

My love, please don't allow the sadness,

To root in the soul's garden!

Spring is there,

With its green eyes inside the bursting buds,

In the shoots that with their fragile heads

  Are pushing the soil,

Spring is there

No one can stop the birds

From flying and singing…

And I am there,

With the first morning breeze,

And the scorched sigh of the sunset,

With my lips venting the dreams' flowers…

My love, don't,

Don't allow the sadness to root in the soul's garden!

Spring is there...

(Mar 2020)

VOICE OF THE HEART

If you ever hear a voice, at midnight,

During those late hours when the being quarrels with

itself,

Stop and hold your breath for a moment,

It's my soul that used to kiss your nights, madly…

Lower your sword, the proud shield,

Engraved let the triumphs be all over it,

Listen to the heart, the tired soldier

That halfway down the road seeks peace…

Empty are the great mausoleums,

The monolith memorials get chewed by time,

The days shrink and the nights stretch,

The glories don't offer rest, only loud cries…

(Apr 2020)

UNTIL WHEN

With their own hands they spread the seed of death,

Like the bad weed that chokes the fields of life,

The bells rang, "it's war time" they said,

But gave us no swords, no shields…

Isolated we strengthen our patience,

And sharpen our hatred day and night,

On the graves that we couldn't throw a handful of dirt,

Our promise, our swear we plant from far…

A war without fronts, no trenches, no sounds of shotguns,

A smokeless Hiroshima, only cries,

With torn lungs humanity moans,

Air! Air! Gasping around the globe, from corner to corner.

An elite will fall and another shall rise,

The table will turn around and change masters,

Until when will people, the silent martyrs

Lay the red carpet with their own bodies for them?

(Apr 2020)

I WILL ALWAYS LOVE YOU

Now, this old temple

Can only give you one thing: Rest!

Take it! The little old raft can always flip over,

The sea can never be trusted

Even though we love it to the last drop…

Open the drawers of my soul,

Get out of them the most beautiful days,

Hang on the gloomy windowsills the kisses and smiles,

While the sky with madness squeezes

All the hidden tears in the clouds…

My love, this tired beat

Is what is left inside my heart,

Take it! You might need it along the road,

On the slopes and uphills that change over without

prairies,

I will always love you…

(Apr 2020)

EMPTINESS

You didn't come…

The wait got cold on the silent windowsill,

On fragile shoulders froze the rime,

The foggy warmth of the dreams…

It waited for the day and saw it off, numb,

Until the eyes grew dark,

The road and the night

Became one inside of them…

From the dark well

The dreams drank the disappointment,

Fake turned out to be the moon's lake,

An endless hole of emptiness...

(May 2020)

I'LL ALWAYS BE THERE

A verse rocks your boat now

As you wander in the sea of dreams,

With the beat of the heart move the oars,

The long lashes on the sleepy eyelids…

You wander and I gently whisper

Watch out there, my love,

Here are the sirens, here is the witch

And here is where Odyssey remained a captive,

Captive to the lust and to the excessive women...

There, in that narrow passage hangs the world,

And other doors open down below with noise,

Deep there on its chest, the waves sing ballads

With Orpheus' lyre as he sleeps for centuries…

Then on your chest I lay my head,

To your waves I surrender in silence,

Captive in storms' hands if you fall, with you I'll be,

A lantern, a rock I will be, until I can't wake up any

more…

(Apr 2020)

WHEN I MISS YOU

53

When I miss you

I can just close my eyes

And under my eyelids you take your path,

Inside my heart I hear your footsteps,

I hear your breathing,

While it wanders in my lungs…

On the open chest

The waves of sighs crash,

And on my lips

Arrive only the sweat interjections,

Your voice that calls me in my dreams…

Who said that I'm alone?

(Apr 2020)

COSMIC SUICIDE

At the end of the day, the sun drowned,

Without any sound, no cries, simply suicide…

The waves carried the bad news to the shore,

Nothing else...

A pale moon from grief

Hung itself, exactly there…

It had not heard about the rebirth,

And couldn't even wait for tomorrow…

The waves carried the bad news to the shore,

Endless sighs,

Cosmic suicide,

Nothing else…

(Apr 2020)

STEAL ME AWAY TONIGHT

Steal me away tonight!

The moon is not out and no one can see us,

The street is empty

And sleepless are my eyes over it...

Steal me away tonight!

The window is open

And hung on the sill, the rope of the dreams

Waits for you just like every night...

Steal me away tonight

In their ballrooms let the stars shake,

All that I need are your eyes

And the drums of the heart that awaits you...

(Apr 2020)

TIMES ROLL IN SINS

Out loud laughs and mocks us MacBeth,

As we endlessly wash our hands, madly,

Other hands sinned again,

But other hands are thinning under water…

Yeah, that's how the baffling times roll over,

Along the crooked path that humanity drags its feet,

Around we go, like a dog gone mad after its tail,

When that darn flee it can't grab by the throat…

(Apr 2020)

I DON'T CARE AT ALL

On the tree's branches the night hung the words of the

day,

Thousands of whispers

That refused to sleep,

Fine, there let them wait the day again,

Together with the new stories

Of the moonlit spies…

I don't care at all,

Let the whispers go wild,

With you I laid down and with you I woke up,

With you I measured the streets

Again one by one…

(May 2020)

LOST IS THE PEACE

Lost is the peace tonight, my love,

Under the tearing waves of a roaring sky over the sea,

The past trembles, the future fears the road,

The gone mad present, searches for its crumbs over the

rocks and cliffs…

I'm sorry my love, lost is the peace,

The murdered life, can't stop crying tonight,

I hold you in my arms, but can't hush the wounds,

Inside the chest the pain roars…

(May 2020)

I DON'T HAVE YOU BESIDE ME...

I don't have you beside me...
In front of me, the table
Is full of emptiness,
Lots and lots of it…
The television and internet fill the background,
With distant smoke puffs of gray grief.
Far and near...a mix of worlds,
And I, live here and there at the same time,
For quite some time…
I don't have you beside me…
And tonight I feel that distances
Are spreading even bigger,
Like two lips of a wound that tear violently apart,
Instead of closing together.
Inside my heart, the moon that's hidden by the clouds,
Drops secretly the tears of a far away sadness,
And I try not let my voice betray me
As I wake you up, my love...
Ah, how I miss you! How much...!
Smoke puffs of gray news
Fog the eyes of my dreams…
(May 2019)

REMEMBER THAT
I LOVE YOU

When the words play with your soul, unintentionally,

Please, remember that I love you,

Calm me down, like you would calm a child

When fearing the darkness…

Hold me in your arms and tell me you are not leaving…

And when the words become stones

And I stumble and fall…

Remember that I love you,

Kiss my torn knees

And the tears in the eyes that cry and shine for you,

Hold me in your arms, like you would hold a child

And tell me that you are not leaving!

Whatever the words say

Listen to my heart, that can't lie to you,

Its whispers and calls for you

Inside of it, listen!

Remember that I love you,

Don't go!

(May 2019)

THE STONES OF SILENCE

The minutes and the hours without you

I gathered in the quarry of my soul,

Impossible to swallow they were,

A mountain they became inside…

The days and weeks, what could I do with them?

Walls of nights, impossible to climb over,

That keep the sleep

Thousands of kilometers away from the eyes…

Come, because I don't know what to do with the months,

The stones of silence

Are taking roots inside of my soul...

(Apr 2019)

DON'T NEED TO BE AWAY

I don't need to be away
To miss you,
As time runs the flowers wither,
Your eyes I need to feel on my body…

The hours steal away, the days steal away,
Stealing the kisses away with them,
Longingness burns the soul like lightning,
"Stay" it says "don't let go of me!"

I don't need to be away
To miss you,
When for a moment I lose you in the fog,
My heart skips a beat…

THE HELL WITH ITHACA

Lose yourself in my eyes this obscure night,

Don't you see, the sea inside them is getting larger,

The ships of dreams are setting sail,

One by one on the strong waves…

There are still dreams inside the tear drops…

The hell with Ithaca, where the devils eat and drink,

And all the rampant throne contenders!

Come my love, there is no other land, a second Ithaca,

But the deep sea inside my eyes,

Let me give to you, for eternity…

(May 2020)

DON'T BE AFRAID!

My love, don't' be afraid

Of the silence that invites you to a lonely waltz,

Inside my silence I stretch my arms, too,

And inside my heart the walls crumble,

    And the abyss fall...

Don't be afraid of this dream, the fearful awake,

The screams of death in the nights and days,

Inside your soul look for me, that's where I am,

A little light fighting the shadows…

Don't be afraid my love,

Of this silence that invites you to a lonely waltz,

In the silence, my arms and my heartbeat you'll find,

Together we are in this crazy waltz...

(May 2020)

YOU'RE THERE

You're there when pain devastates my soul,

Ripping my wound's crusts without mercy,

You're there, at the edge of the cliff,

When towards the flames they push me,

With their looks saying to me:

  "Take one more step!"

You're there, inside my tired heart,

A rhythm, a hidden pulse you have become,

Inside my veins, you ripped the requiem of my dark days,

And a new song you're giving to my blood…

(May 2019)

JUST COME

Just come!

A night without diamonds and a moon necklace give me,

A dark well, let the sky be,

A gray morning let it bring tomorrow…

Just come!

The coffee shall await us, already made in the morning,

The table will hold our heads

   Upon our elbows and sighs…

Just come!

Don't hesitate to take your steps,

I know how to keep you close to me

   Even when you're silent,

     Even when you're tired...

(May 2020)

IN DREAMS AND MEMORIES

During the night I run after the fireflies of memories,

To find you, the light in the endless darkness,

To wrap you in my arms and to fall asleep,

Lying in the midst of the ether that rocks us together…

The clouds run somnambulant, the leaves rave,

The bedsheets moan under their breath while sleeping,

The heart's tremble doesn't know where to stop,

In the dreams or in the memories that rush like a river…

(Jun 2020)

LIKE MANY OTHERS

You too, betrayed yourself,

Ordinarily, like many others

That get tired and forget to live,

Inside the character they've crafted…

On the path of the flash you betrayed yourself,

Randomly, just like all the others! I don't blame you!

Hard is the road of the soul,

Strong is the temptation in every crossroad…

It will take some time, but I'll forgive you, love,

Even though, you'll never ask the heart forgiveness,

You won't have time, you'll be busy, as always,

A magician in the creation of the next illusion…

(Jun 2022)

KNOCK ON MY MORNING

Knock on my morning,

And send away the crazy dream,

Bring the scary chase to an end

In the thick woods where darkness resides…

From the bottom of the silence send me a word,

And together with it, your heart,

To give me a breath of air and fire…

To burn the tear like the dew on the flowers

When the sun comes down and kisses it with longing…

So the wait and the icy night may be forgotten,

On the lips of the morning, burning out slowly…

(May 2020)

ABANDONMENT IN SILENCE

Everyone has left,

Leaving me the mess of the finished feast,

And the bitter silence…

Somewhere else, perhaps they drink their second cup of

coffee,

Or perhaps, they start the ritual all over again,

Because, that's how the world is…

And you, just like me,

Sitting down by the empty table of the soul,

Face to face with the mess and the silence…

That's how the world is split, my love,

With one side the guests that eat, drink and leave,

And on the other, the abandoned hosts…

Stretch your fingers and find my hand,

It's there, lying in the emptiness,

    Waiting…

(May 2020)

UNFORTUNATELY

Nothing will happen after the first glass

Nor after the second one,

The words won't spread over the table,

The hands won't look to find each-other…

The feelings will hurt even more,

Banging on the closed doors,

Maybe, somewhere, after the third glass,

The temples will start beating loud like the heart…

The feelings don't get drunk, or slumber amazingly,

Not even after the fourth glass,

The poisoned blood, even more, unfortunately,

Will continue to love you in silence…

(May 2022)

Armenida Qyqja

I WANT TO BE SILENT TONIGHT

My love, I don't want to talk tonight,

The world has tired me out, tantalized me,

With the noise of its words it has drowned me...

Tonight I just need you to hold me,

Like an infant that can't stop crying,

Distant, remote let everything be…

I am tired of the world,

Day after day with lies, disappointments,

Word after word of poison in the blood and pain…

My love, don't worry!

Tonight, on your chest I just want to be silent,

Outside let the noisy words remain…

(Jun 2020)

YOU CAME TO ME

You came to me with the warm rain of longingness in your eyes,

With the heat of the earth on a summer day on your lips,

You came to me with hugs of the days,

And the nights, wrapped in your arms,

The distance became an infant cradled by kisses…

You came to me and all my pores,

Called your name feverishly while dreaming,

The feelings woke up and then returned to the dream,

The biggest, sweetest dream…

Love…

(Jun 2019)

I WILL ALWAYS LOVE YOU

Now, this old temple

Can only give you one thing: Rest!

Take it! The little old raft can always flip over,

The sea can never be trusted

Even though we love it to the last drop…

Open the drawers of my soul,

Get out of them the most beautiful days,

Hang on the gloomy windowsills the kisses and smiles,

While the sky with madness squeezes

All the hidden tears in the clouds…

My love, this tired beat

Is what is left inside my heart,

Take it! You might need it along the road,

On the slopes and uphills that change over without

valleys,

I will always love you…

(Apr 2020)

YOU LOVE ME

You love all the colors of my voice,

And the eyes that hide in the corners,

Behind the fogy curtains,

Unsuccessfully trying to intercept the tears

You love me…

You love me even when I become a crazy wind,

Raging and then calming down in your soul,

Like the air I let myself fly up and then I drop down,

Because I know, for me you keep your arms open…

I know, you love all my colors,

Even the gray that invades me and turns me into a child,

You hold me in your arms and with endless kisses,

The woman in me you wake up again…

(Jun 2019)

DREAMS AND LONGINGNESS

You sleep…, thousands of kilometers away from me,
In my mind,
A bed of longingness, the soft clouds become for you,
My kisses,
The pillow under your sleepy head.
You sleep…, so far and near me,
My love...

My head, swarmed by thoughts,
I lay near you,
Beyond the distances…
And with closed eyelids I watch
How the night fades in silence,
And the stars from far away
Drip lights and dreams on them.
You sleep…, so far and near me,
My love...
(Jun 2019)

DON'T BE JEALOUS

Don't be jealous my love,

Of the eyes that look at me from far,

Dogs and wolves howl at the moon

Through centuries of loneliness,

But no one managed to lay in bed with it...

Don't be jealous, my love,

Of the wind that blows,

Just indulging the leaves,

The words it brings, takes back with it,

Because my soul lives on your breath only...

(Jun 2020)

Armenida Qyqja

IN YOUR EYES' DREAM

Sneaky thoughts play with the silence,

Like the curtains play with the wind,

From the open window, they keep the hope hanging,

Shivering in caresses, but yet not giving in…

I untied all of them, removed the clips,

The vises that held tight their gateways,

To the ether I gave them, to take in its arms,

In your eyes' dream to plant me…

(Jun 2020)

MY LONGINGNESS AWAITS YOU

Inside the frames, with a thin pencil,

I enclose your kisses every day,

Upon my small lips,

Your lips, waiting to receive them again…

Black, heavy boundaries I place on the waitings,

Inside the eyes, they are clear-glass lakes,

Endless horizons, may stretch out there,

My longingness, my love, awaits only you, inside…

You look at me every day from the mirror,

With the sweet silence, like you used to do,

I smile at you while crying inside,

With your kisses filling the spaces…

(Jun 2019)

Armenida Qyqja

I LOVED YOU EVEN MORE

Full of ups and downs is life,

Elbows, meddlings, lid open sewers,

But you should know that I if admired you on your

heights,

Fallen, I loved every little bit of you!

I never measured success by the victories,

Because sometimes crawlers win,

Those that never stretch their step,

But web their slime of praise and intrigue…

I loved you more with every fall,

Because you got up on your feet again,

Holding your heart in your hand,

Making your way out of this swamp, full of scum…

(Jun 2020)

NO TIME TO HOLD A GRUDGE

I don't have time to hold a grudge,

To play games like other women do,

There's a school that I didn't attend in my early youth,

Too late now to run after that kind of diploma…

I don't have room in my heart, for yesterday's anger,

Full are all the crevices with pain,

Some kisses you lay on them,

Band-aids, to hold the cracked walls…

(Jul 2020)

WAKE ME UP

I'm waiting for your touch,

To shake from my frozen shoulders

The dust of the ground up silence,

This gray ash, of a choked volcano

That covers my being unwillingly…

Covered up, your kisses sleep feverishly while burning,

Same as yesterday, today, tomorrow…

Even if two thousand years would pass…

But don't wait any longer, come touch me!

From the long somnolence shake

The day and the night that have fallen in the eyes…

Stretch your fingers over my hair!

Let the unraveled world tremble a little

By the burning fire,

Let them say "Pompeii woke up again"...

(Jul 2020)

STARS OF DREAMS

Longingness fills your silhouette,

That comes near me, light like air each night,

Inside the heart dips the paint brush,

And fills all the spaces with kisses…

Your eyes and your lips get fuller

And so do the arms that used to hold me next to the chest,

In the choked silence, I hear your heartbeat

And a thousand words that only she can say…

A river of light you become, rushing all over me,

And there's no line that can keep you in,

I close my eyes and I feel your lips on my forehead,

Stars of dreams light my darkness each night...

(Jul 2020)

Armenida Qyqja

UNDER THE PRINTS OF KISSES AND WAITINGS

How can I hide the sad melody of my breath,

So close to you, how can I?

This autumn etude that is playing on its way,

Wets your sleepy image

With the tears that hold strong within the shores…

On my chest, I rock your dreams,

As loneliness awaits us both outside,

This autumn etude that plays on its way,

How many moans and cries hides

Deep under the prints of kisses and waitings…

(Sep 2020)

AUTUMN DOESN'T HOLD HER STEPS

I smile at the mirror and she falls for the lies,

The lie of the beauty casted by a ray of light

Upon the last flower left in the garden,

Upon the droplets of dew that lock inside the desires of a

life…

It falls for the lies, and for the thousand time,

Tries to smile to itself while tearing through the smiles…

On the wrinkled forehead of the sky, the rainbows

explode,

But autumn doesn't hold her steps…

(Sep 2020)

I'M NOT LOST

In the tearful eye of sky search for me, my love,

I am there. I'm not lost…

Under the gloomy grays,

The clouds can't hide my footprints…

And my voice can't be drowned by autumn's moans…

From the soul's warm nest

Falls free, with thousands chirpings,

Even though the birds are long gone…

Search for me, my love, search! I'm not lost…

From the cradle where the dream rocks,

Like in fairy tales, I wait for your longing eyes,

With the light of the east to shine on me…

(Sep 2020)

EUROPE IN MOURNING

Some bangs made your sleepy columns tremble

And the Eiffel tower with shaky knees

Asked you anxiously: "What's happening?"

You rubbed your eyes, Europe,

The heads were not made of marble

And the bangs didn't come from the ending autumn's

sky…

In mourning, the statues lowered their heads, from Louvre

to Vienna,

And the violins hushed their bows in the parks,

This time, impregnated with all sorts of viruses,

Why does it beckon death from edge to edge, so lustfully...

(Nov 2020)

LONELY NIGHT

Cold is the breath of the evening tonight,

Over the ground lays alone and turns herself into tears.

No one hears her…

In their beds, people sleep…

Tomorrow with heavy steps they'll walk over her,

Lost in their thoughts…

As always, people don't notice anything,

Other than it's cold…

(Oct 2020)

THE DAY KEEPS GROWING INSIDE US

We have surpassed the edges of craziness,

Just like Odyssey, tied up to the mast,

And we, holding tight to one word,

Dared to release ourselves in the open sea…

Let the world talk bad about us now,

Old news we'll become to her tomorrow,

But today, today my love, the day is growing,

Inside of us it's becoming a century...

(Nov 2020)

Armenida Qyqja

I LOVE YOU EVEN MORE

Don't fear the darkness inside my eyes,

The eclipses, when sun's road to the heart is blocked,

I love you even more when the light is put out by the tear,

With you in my soul, the prayers and hopes I light up

again…

Don't fear the lips, locked in silence,

The rivers of words, just sleep for a short while,

With your return, they'll wake up again, love,

Towards the sea of your eyes, they'll flow with outburst

joy, as always…

(Nov 2020)

LIVE

My love, pick up your pieces and live!

We all have been torn by the world,

Through the hands of our most loved ones,

That's why it hurts hundreds of times more…

Pick up your pieces

And take the path of trust again,

Even though, it was on that path you were ambushed,

On the most beautiful day…

Pick up your pieces and continue,

Because you can't change, my love,

You were born like this,

A stranger, in a world of chameleons…

(Nov 2020)

Armenida Qyqja

MAKE A SOUND

Come and make a sound for this night,

That is cracking with such stupidity,

In self admiration over the frozen pond of loneliness!

Awaken her! Enough of her pride

With me, a silenced prisoner, inside of her…

Make a sound tonight!

And if you can't,

Even just the sounds of your breath

Would suffice to crumble the glass walls

That keep me away from you…

Come, make a sound

And bring me back to myself again…

(Nov 2020)

MUTINY

Like thinned, malnourished cattle, graze the thoughts

On the naked field,

Chewing and regurgitating the few strands of grass

They find here and there, under the frost…

They lie to the jaws, the empty stomach

And try to weave dreams

About tomorrow's abundance,

The ray of sun upon the lush green…

Come my love! Save me!

I can't lie to myself any more,

Without you, all my body parts,

Have gone to mutiny, a long time ago...

(Nov 2020)

Armenida Qyqja

WHERE ARE YOUR FINGERS

The curtains fell.

Dark, heavy…

Now, I need your hands to push them aside

So that the light can enter my eyes again…

Where are your fingers,

Where are they wandering, lost,

'Till yesterday they used to play sweetly with my hair,

As I lay my head on the dreams…

Where are they

As I need them to take me by the hand,

To speak to my heart, to say: Don't be afraid,

It's just a Night

That will be followed by the Day…

Where are your fingers tonight…

(Nov 2020)

HOW SOON WE FORGET

How many apocalypses has the world endured?

One more horrible than the other,

Each one has only cried his own end,

Licking only his own wounds…

This shadow of death too shall pass,

Hiding behind the curtain that it came from,

And we, as always, will forget the terror,

Chasing the same path of hell exactly…

Stubborn, hard rock headed this humankind keeps rolling,

Unchanged even from the atomic bombs,

With its own hands, embroids its own coffin,

And then it cries, as it starts to feel the pain inside of it...

(Dec 2020)

THE WISH BANK

The fountain has frozen together with the wishes,

I keep throwing coins in it,

A wish above all wishes, to awaken the wishes,

That sleep with the winter in your eyes...

The heart doesn't give up, as long as it has a beat,

The blood that gurgles sweetly your name,

While giving all its warmth to your being,

The air that surrounds your body...

Midwinter, but the heart spins dreams,

Wishes upon wishes, endlessly,

All in one single bank deposit,

In the one you added my name with prayers...

(Jan 2022)

LET IT COME...

The first cherry blossom is blooming,

In my far away city, spring is trying to arrive...

Like a bud that really wants to bloom,

In my eye, the kiss cries silently...

Let it come! Gone you won't be able

To do to me, what she'll do to the cherries,

One by one, till the end of the ally,

That hardly gets enough of life's sun...

Let it come! Let it come! I surrender,

On its valleys I'll lay down,

I'll let the sun place his lips on your kisses,

I know, I'll still feel cold, even when it will be summer...

(Mar 2022)

THERE'S NO TIME

I don't have time for the train cars full of words,

Your undecided thoughts on their rusted platforms,

In the century of atom and cosmic ships,

The moment is not something to be lost…

Time goes by with giant steps,

Even though nothing changes in your minds,

Life just passes you by,

As everything spins around the latest iPhone…

Away migrates the gaze, the heartbeat,

On the path that winds up with the wind without return,

At the last frontiers, empty you'll find yourself,

Your eyes praying to life as you do to God…

(July 2022)

SMALL ARE THE WORDS

Mankind has made love,

Even before Sappho was born,

Long, long time before that, my love

Close your eyes and like a blind man

Run your fingertips upon heart's trembles…

Chase the gasping breath, beyond the lips,

As it crashes to the bottom of the soul,

Like two illiterate people, let us surrender to the kisses,

Fearless for the words that have abandoned us…

Let them go, all of them,

Together with their ancient codes,

Small are the words,

Where the heart's thunder crushes…

(July 2022)

RIDING THE HORSES OF THE WIND

The trotting sounds inside your heart, listen!

Riding the horses of the wind I'll come at night,

With the rhythm of the beats they'll knock on the clouds,

Ending the run on the white pillow.

I'll come and I'll tear down the curtain of tears,

That keeps the moon's light from your eyes,

On my back I'll carry the hidden dawn,

Flaming petals I'll lay on your bed.

Riding the horses of the wind I'll come, my love,

With my hair down and mad run,

I'll stop nowhere, my breath I'll hold,

To lay my head on your barren chest…

(Aug 2019)

A KISS I WILL BE...

When my body like a wasted fire-pan will be,

Come and gently stir the ash on my lips with your finger,

The eyes that gave you their last glow,

Will feel your touch beneath the dark char..

My love, do come closer and breathe on me,

Do not fear air will take me away,

Over your shoulders, your hair, crumbled down

A soft kiss I will be full of longingness…

(Sep 2019)

WITHOUT YOUR KISS

An orphan I've become without your kiss,

During the night that spins like a trap around me,

To you I call, but my voice gets lost in the abyss,

Around my throat pain twists about like a loop.

I wait for you sitting on the pavements of feelings,

To come and raise me up, on my feet again,

The beautiful dream to put on my eyes again,

To lighten the stars, to vanish the clouds.

An orphan I've become without your kiss,

Like an abandoned infant on a doorstep,

The child and the woman inside me, are waiting for you,

In your warm arms to keep us…

(Sep 2019)

WITHOUT YOU

Like a statue that sleeps under the ground,

Without your kiss I am left,

Forgotten by time in centuries of silence,

Unseen, untouched by the sun's light.

Undone, faded are now my contours

That your eye's chisel carved, my love.

Deaf emptiness drops its tears

On the face you once made beautiful.

Nothing, nothing I am, without your gaze,

The kiss that wakes up the day in my eyes,

Only endless night and dreamless sleep,

Invades every space deep within my being…

(July 2019)

LIKE ATLANTIS I AM

I released the boats of my feelings

In the deep ocean of your eyes,

The white masts took the wind

From your warm lips, full of love.

A single drop of water, a wave,

Inside your eye, a storm I am,

An endless hug in time,

That engulfs your fragile soul.

My love, in the ocean of your heart

I sail and rest like the lost Atlantis,

A world that sleeps for thousands of years,

By your kisses and the breeze covered…

(Apr 2019)

COME

I look at you and inside the tense nerves

A feeling is counting down the seconds…

I smile…You don't know, that just a touch

Would be enough for it to jump at you…

We walk… upon millions of neurons,

A mine field within every centimeter square,

Madness, of course even the heart knows it's madness

And still it doesn't want to stop loving you…

What difference would it make

If only crazy people did crazy things?!

Identical twins would be the events and the days,

Trust me, the surprises would tire out…Come!

(Jun 2022)

DON'T SEARCH FOR THE WORDS

A moment broke free from the chains of time,

The iron mechanism of its heart,

Arrhythmic suddenly the breathing of the night,

As it couldn't get enough air through the lungs…

The darkness couldn't hide the light in yours eyes,

The sparks that flew all around,

With the words that stole away from your lips,

From you to me, during the night they migrated…

Don't search for their babblings,

Their nest they have built inside of me,

To the other edge of the world my darling,

With my soul like a ship, I'll carry them…

(JUN 2022)

ON YOUR CHEST

From far away, the drops of nectar will scold me,

As they drip from the ripe grapes

With the voice of the unmade wine from the vineries,

"Why didn't you wait a little longer?" they'll say to me…

The leaves of the trees in the garden will scold me

And I'll blush like fire, way in the distance,

It will be fall in my soul by then,

I left before the storks, in summer's peak…

Your longingness will forgive me and will take me to the

chest,

One by one hushing summer's scoldings,

Kneeling them down to the heart,

That loves me as it never did before…

(July 2022)

Armenida Qyqja

PASS THE CLOUDS

I'm with you on those dusty paths,

That your tired memory wanders,

Hundreds of by passers, faces,

The heart is searching for the familiar footsteps…

I'm with you when the clouds break the paths

And the horizons shatter in front of your eyes,

When the words lose their way through the storm,

In the sucking whirlpools of silence…

I'm with you behind the closed doors,

On the knocks that fall to floor unanswered,

On the bed that loneliness lies awake,

Thousands of prayers I've turned into sheet spreads…

Forsake the mazes and get beyond the clouds,

A path to the sun may the heart flourish,

Take my fist and knock again,

Let the waiting shake from the sleeping doors…

(July 2021)

YOU HAVE ME WITH YOU

A handful of dreams I'm leaving on your sky clear eyes,

So that they can lower the sun on their lashes that I love,

With their wings they'll chase away the clouds,

Talk about me to your heart…

Remember my laughter anytime

That the rains pour, heavy with longingness,

Over the heartbeat start pacing calmly,

Somewhere deep in there, I know, you have me…

Understand my love, I haven't gone anywhere,

For as long as you keep me, tight in your blood,

To give air to your heart with each drop,

As time flows into the aorta, day after day…

(July 2022)

Armenida Qyqja

NOTHING MORE OR LESS

That is love, my darling,

Nothing more or less,

A breath that holds on the thirsty lip,

A kiss that sweetly puts the soul to sleep…

And suddenly, the fear abandons the heart,

Just like the shadows when the sun enters it,

Edge to edge the light fills the eyes,

From the heart that starts beating harder…

That's the miracle, life's secrete,

Nothing more or less,

No one can teach it to you except the heart,

Where your soul takes shelter during the storm…

(July 2022)

HIDDEN YOU KEEP YOUR HEARTBEAT

The messages spread endlessly in the galaxies,

In every known language, even made up ones,

While I, can't find a single word,

That can speak to your heart, so close to mine…

I exhausted all the words and the why's,

On the paths where I wander with your shadow only,

As I couldn't split myself in two,

To speak for you, to give them the answers…

Mankind keeps trying restlessly,

There among the stars, others alike to find,

While I look you in the eyes, but can't feel your heart,

Hidden somewhere you keep its beats…

(May 2022)

Armenida Qyqja

FOR YOUR EYES ONLY

Without any masts the dream ships are left,

Torn to tiny pieces by time,

The sea is not to be blamed, only the strong wind,

Raging waves and storms keeps brewing…

Inside your eyes, with longingness float

White pieces of cloth, in the infinite blue,

The hearts like to wander with desire,

With the dreams to sleep and wake up endlessly…

Just the tired arms are left now, my love

And the heartbeat that loves you as it did before,

Above the waves, the tired ship is letting go,

To gather the dreams, for your eyes, only…

(Jun 2022)

AMONG THOUSAND WHISPERS

Don't worry, stay calm my love,

A moment's craziness turned you into a hero,

There are no hydras, Medusa died a long time ago,

There's only solitude that eats at me in silence…

Don't worry at all my love,

Uneaten will the smile remain

And this eye, where your image hides,

That's how love is…

If you can, come my love, come,

There in the world of my fairytales,

Where the heart is always waiting for you

Among thousands of heartbeats and whispers…

(Jun 2021)

DON'T LET THE LIGHT
MISS YOU

Come, abandon the world of solitude and come,

There, where my voice calls you even in your sleep,

Don't fear yourself anymore,

Deep in there, I live now…

Forget the failures, the betrayals, the abysses,

The Circes with thousand magic tricks and games,

I'm not like anything the world has seen before,

I get my power only from my heart…

Come my love, don't let the light miss you,

On the path in paves between the eyes,

Come, let's add another miracle, to the world,

That drowns itself in hate and tears…

(July 2022)

TAKE ME IN

Take me inside your temple,

There, where the most sacred words are whispered,

Where even silence has its valued place,

Sitting close to the burning desires…

Take me in with the breath, the light of the eyes,

There, where you've never let anyone in!

Inside your dreams, your thoughts,

In silence let me in, my love…

I promise, I won't touch or change a thing,

In its holy place let each comma remain,

Take me in with the breath I release over you,

A kiss may I become, inside your temple…

(Jun 2021)

THE ONE I LOVED THE MOST

Surrounded by Judas I've always been,

But you were the one I loved above all,

Dressed as my heart's best friend,

Undetected you came in and named the feeling…

The wounds hurt whenever the wind blows,

The change of seasons, hurts even more,

The trees dress and undress themselves in pain,

Like them I die and come to life, again and again…

Lies are the words and even the silence,

The kisses that used to put me to sleep,

Surrounded by Judas, I've always been,

But you were the one I loved the most…

(Jun 2022)

LOVE DOESN'T WEAR PATCHED UP CLOTHES

Torn to pieces is our story,

With us pulling on opposite ends,

Useless to stitch it up with words and promises,

Love doesn't wear patched up clothes…

Go now, where you've been heading for, since long time

ago,

Take the bigger piece to yourself,

You will need it my dear, to make light for you,

Sun to become, when cold you'll feel in the world…

Go, where you've been gone with your mind,

You can't conceal the noise of your steps to the heart,

You've been missing for a long time now,

In my eyes you don't look at yourself anymore…

(Jun 2022)

AWAKE MY TIME

Like Giaconda in the museum, I'm waiting,
Completely lost in another world…
The light of your eyes to fall on me,
So that I can take shape and form and live again…

The world keeps searching in vain for the secret,
Hidden deep in the eyes and the lips,
No one knows to whom the kiss belongs,
Sealed on them, with eternity's stamp…

Come then, throw some eye-light on me,
Shape and form, give me, bring me back to life,
With your kiss, wake up the time,
That sleeps inside of me for centuries…
(Jun 2021)

NO MORE HEARTACHE

You don't change, neither do I,

Not one letter, one stop, one comma,

Whole, I want my love,

To have me its light, its heartbeat…

You won't grow up, though you're turning gray,

I can't teach you to listen to my breathing,

In front of my eyes, you lose yourself in emptiness,

It's useless to wait, to hope in us…

Gone you are again, before even coming,

My heart tells me and there's no more heartache,

Well, I grew up…you forced me to grow up,

I understood, love, I was loving, alone…

(May 2022)

UNTOUCHABLE

Keep your secrets to yourself,

I don't want to know anything from the past,

You won't find me in her temples,

My arms need only freedom…

Give me only your soul through your lips,

Just like it came, as a child on this earth,

Its sacredness let it find again through the kisses,

The most beautiful prayer in this world…

Our time starts now, love,

The counting of the steps inside the heart,

Nothing exists before that,

You are untouchable, under the shield of feelings…

(Aug 2022)

ABOUT THE AUTHOR

Armenida Qyqja was born in Tirana, Albania in 1977 and immigrated to Canada in 1995. She is the author of five poetry books: "Beyond the rails of rain", "Letters without envelopes", "Between the heart beats", "Kisses in ether", "Forty plus" and is the process of releasing another poetry book as well as her first book of short stories and novels. "A bunch of poems instead of flowers" is her first attempt to bring her poetry to the English readers.